What are rainforests?

Rainforests are made up of tall trees and many other plants, all growing thickly together. They cover huge areas of land. It is always hot and damp inside a rainforest so plants keep growing all year round. Rainforests are home to the greatest variety of plants and animals in the world. People live there too.

▽ The Amazon rainforest is the largest in the world.

Where are rainforests?

Most rainforests grow in hot wet parts of the world called the **tropics**. The tropics are near the **equator**. The equator is an imaginary line around the middle of the earth, where the weather is warmest. Tropical rainforests are only found in countries near the equator.

Do you live in a tropical area?

▷ This rainforest is on a tropical island.

Areas of rainforest

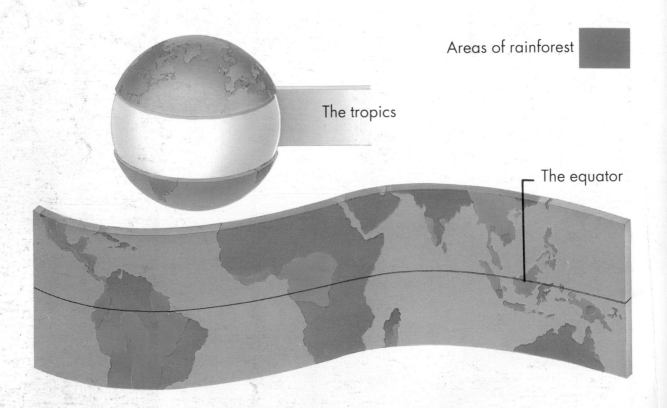

The tropics

The equator

4

What are rainforests like?

It is hot and gloomy, and often wet, inside a rainforest. Many forest trees are very tall and grow close together. Their leaves and branches act like an umbrella which blocks out the strong sunlight. This thick top layer of leaves and branches is called the forest **canopy**. Shorter trees and other plants grow under the canopy in-between the taller trees.

Canopy

The canopy is the top layer of the forest. It gets almost all the sunlight and rainfall.

Understorey

The understorey is a place of shade. Very little sunlight reaches the plants that grow here.

Forest floor

Very little grows on the dark forest floor. It is always covered with fallen leaves, flowers and twigs.

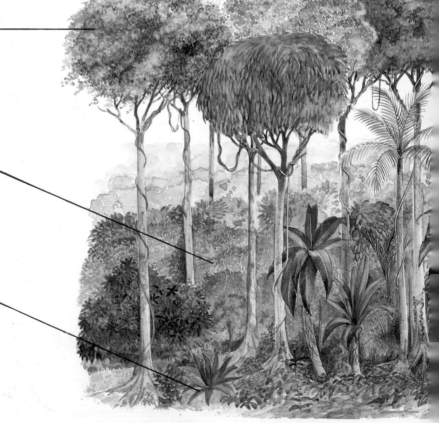

Emergents

A few very tall trees stand out high above the canopy. They are called emergents.

What is the weather like?

Rainforests are hot and wet all year round. The trees help to make the rain. Big roots soak up water from the ground. The water is sucked up through the trunk into the leaves. The heat makes the water in the leaves **evaporate** into the air. This **water vapour condenses** to make clouds. Rainclouds make rain fall onto the forest again.

▷ The air inside a rainforest feels warm and damp.

▽ There are often heavy rainstorms which leave forest plants dripping with water.

8

Plants

Trees are the largest rainforest plants. Many rainforest trees have huge roots that show above the ground. These are called **buttress roots**. Many other plants grow underneath the trees. Some plants hang like thick ropes around the trunks and branches. Others live on the bark of the tree trunks. Many rare and unusual flowering plants grow in rainforests.

▷ The climbing pepper vine grows over other plants in sunlit clearings.

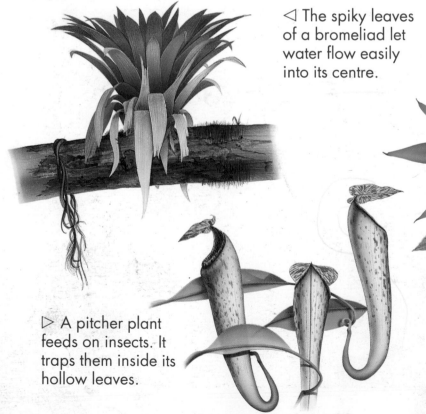

◁ The spiky leaves of a bromeliad let water flow easily into its centre.

▷ A pitcher plant feeds on insects. It traps them inside its hollow leaves.

△ The bright colour of this passion flower attracts birds to feed on its nectar.

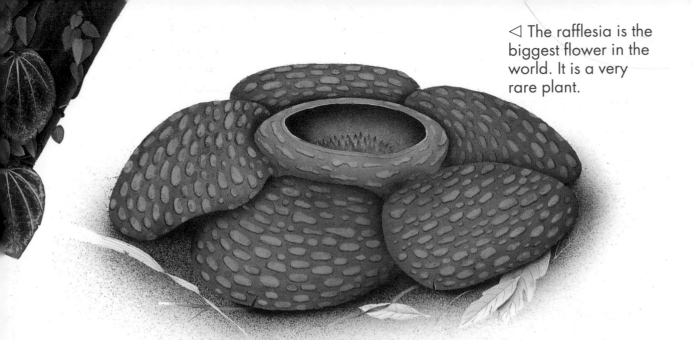

◁ The rafflesia is the biggest flower in the world. It is a very rare plant.

▽ Buttress roots help to support the great weight of these trees.

11

Animals

Animals live at every level of the forest. Some live in the light leafy tree tops where they find food and shelter. Monkeys swing through the canopy. Snakes slither along branches in search of frogs and birds. Jaguars climb up trees to sit on low branches. Some animals stay on the ground, hunting for food near river banks and amongst low plants.

△ The sloth has long claws. They help it to cling on to tree trunks and branches.

▷ The fruit bat sucks the juice from fruits and drops the seeds. It helps to spread the seeds.

▽ The jaguar has a spotty coat. This helps it to hide amongst the trees when it hunts.

▽ The anaconda is one of the world's largest snakes. It lives in or near water.

▷ The spider monkey can hang on to a branch with its tail.

▽ The bright colours of this frog warn other animals that it is poisonous.

△ The orang-utan uses its long arms to swing through the trees.

▷ The tapir uses its nose to pull food nearer its mouth.

Birds

Brightly coloured birds, like the macaw, nest in the trees. They fly from branch to branch in search of food. Some birds are fruit-eaters, and some birds are seed-eaters. Many smaller birds feed on insects or **nectar**. Some birds, like the nightjar, live on the ground. They peck for food on the forest floor.

△ The hummingbird's long thin beak can reach the nectar inside flowers.

▽ The dark colours of the nightjar help it to hide on the forest floor.

▷ The toucan feeds mainly on fruit. It helps to spread the fruit trees' seeds.

▽ The cassowary cannot fly. It is one of the largest rainforest birds.

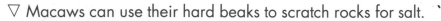

◁ This giant eagle eats monkeys. It nests in the tallest trees.

▽ Macaws can use their hard beaks to scratch rocks for salt.

Minibeasts

Millions of tiny creatures such as insects and spiders live on the trees and in the undergrowth. Beetles, ants and termites crawl amongst the dead leaves on the forest floor. They help to break up this **forest litter**. Butterflies and moths fly between the flowering plants, searching for nectar. They help to spread pollen from flower to flower.

▷ Leaf-cutter ants take leaves to their nests. They use them to make food.

▽ Termites help to clean the forest floor. They feed on dead wood.

▷ This blue morpho butterfly has brown underwings to help it hide amongst leaves.

◁ The bright colours of this shield bug warn attackers that it is poisonous.

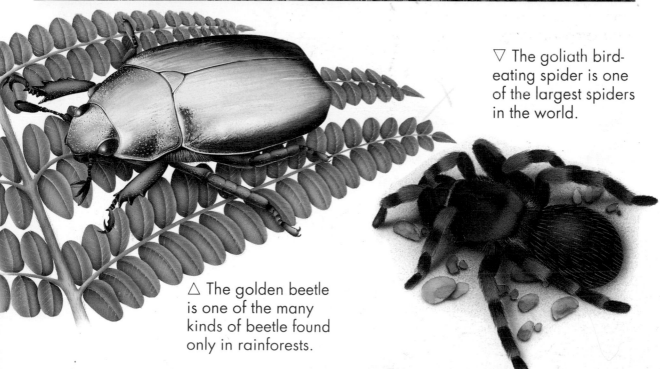

▽ The goliath bird-eating spider is one of the largest spiders in the world.

△ The golden beetle is one of the many kinds of beetle found only in rainforests.

People

People have lived in tropical rainforests for thousands of years. The forest provides them with food, shelter, clothes, tools and medicines. Today there are millions of people living in rainforests around the world. They belong to different groups or **tribes**, each with its own customs.

▷ Many forest tribes live in a village or settlement in a space cleared of trees.

▽ The Kayapo Indians hunt and grow crops in the forests of Brazil.

△ The Baka Pygmies live in the rainforests of West Africa.

△ The Urueu-wau-wau Indians, like many rainforest people, paint their bodies.

How the people live

Rainforest people hunt animals for meat to eat. They also gather berries, fruits and the roots of some plants.

Some tribes clear away trees to make a small space for growing food crops. This is called slash-and-burn farming. The space is farmed for a few years. Then the people move on to a new place. The forest grows back on the land left behind.

▽ Hunters use bows and arrows to reach animals high in the canopy.

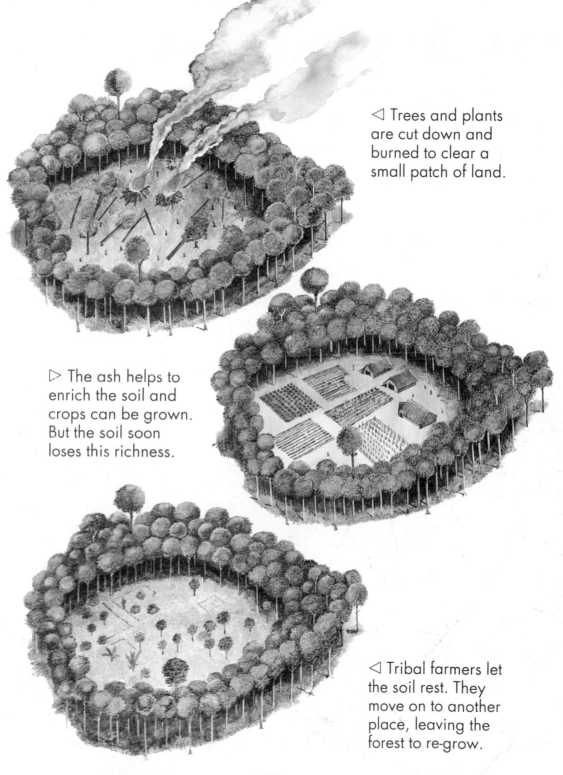

◁ Trees and plants are cut down and burned to clear a small patch of land.

▷ The ash helps to enrich the soil and crops can be grown. But the soil soon loses this richness.

◁ Tribal farmers let the soil rest. They move on to another place, leaving the forest to re-grow.

Surviving in the rainforest

Rainforest people know how to get everything they need from the forest without destroying the trees forever. They know how to prepare roots for eating, and how parts of some plants can be used as medicines. They know which berries are not poisonous and where to find sweet honey in the forest.

▷ Rainforest people get honeycombs from honeybee nests high in the canopy.

▽ Rainforest plants are used to make everyday items such as rope and baskets.

Why we need rainforests

Many of the things we use every day come from rainforests. The trees are important for another reason. Their leaves have tiny holes for breathing. They breathe in **carbon dioxide** from the air. When too many trees are cut down, more carbon dioxide stays in the air. Carbon dioxide traps heat, so the air around the earth gets warmer. This can cause serious problems for the earth.

▽ Many of our medicines come from rainforest plants.

▽ Rattan furniture is made from rainforest plants.

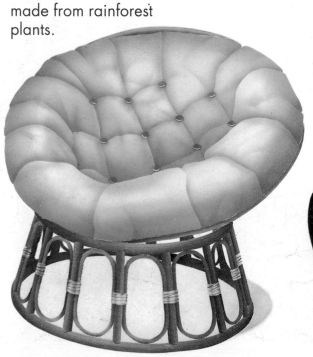

▷ Rainforest rubber is used to make many useful things.

◁ Pineapples and guavas are some of the fruits that grow in rainforests.

▷ Chewing gum is made using chicle from sapodilla or naseberry trees.

▽ Rubber is made from latex collected from rubber trees.

Threats to the rainforest

Thousands of rainforest trees are being cut down or burnt to make space for farmland, roads, buildings or **mines**. Every second an area of rainforest the size of a football pitch is destroyed. When trees are removed rain washes away the soil. Serious floods may occur. Many different plants and animals are losing their homes and becoming **extinct**.

▷ Many trees were destroyed to make this landing strip for airplanes.

▷ Some land is cleared completely for mining minerals such as copper.

△ Trees are also cut down for their wood. It can be sold for a lot of money.

◁ Huge areas of rainforest have been cut down to make way for cattle grazing.

Saving the rainforests

There are many **conservation** groups and charities working to save the world's rainforests. New trees are being planted to replace those that have been destroyed. In some countries there are areas of rainforest which are protected. These **forest reserves** also protect the wildlife. Much more could still be done. Everyone can help.

▷ Many different kinds of trees are being planted to help rainforest conservation.

▽ Many rainforest people are making their own protests against rainforest destruction.

Things to do

- Make a poster to tell people about the importance of rainforests. Put it in your window or in your classroom.

- Visit your nearest botanical garden and enter the tropical house. It is hot and damp inside, like a rainforest.

- Grow your own rainforest plant at home. Plant an avocado stone in compost. Keep it in a light place and water it regularly.

Useful Addresses:

Friends of the Earth
Rainforest Campaign
26-28 Underwood Street
London
N1 7JQ

Rainforest Foundation
2 Ingate Place
Battersea
London
SW8 3NS

World Wide Fund for Nature
Panda House
Weyside Park
Godalming
Surrey
GU7 1XR

Survival International
310 Edgware Road
London
W2 1DY

Glossary

buttress roots Huge roots that develop to support heavy tree trunks and help keep very tall trees upright.

canopy The top layer of leaves and branches in a rainforest.

carbon dioxide A gas that is present in air. Air is made up of a mixture of gases, including oxygen and carbon dioxide. When we breathe our bodies take in oxygen and give out carbon dioxide.

condenses Changes from a gas into a liquid. Clouds are formed when water vapour condenses into very tiny droplets of water.

conservation The protection of plants and animals and their natural homes, and the care of the land.

equator The equator is an imaginary line around the middle of the earth.

evaporate Change from a liquid into a gas.

extinct When every member of a type of animal or plant dies, it is said to be extinct. It is gone forever.

forest litter A layer of dead leaves, twigs and flowers on the forest floor.

forest reserves Areas of forest set apart for the protection of wildlife and nature.

mines Places from which minerals are dug out of the ground. Copper and gold are minerals.

nectar A sugary liquid produced by the flowers of many plants. It is collected by insects and some birds.

tribes Groups of people who share the same social customs and beliefs, and live together in the same area.

tropics The tropics are areas near the equator, on either side of it.

water vapour water in the form of a gas or a very fine mist.

Index

Photographic credits: Bruce
Coleman Ltd (G Cubitt) 11,
(G Ziesler) 15, (L C Marigo) 29;
Ecoscene (D Pearson) 25;
Environmental Picture Library
(S Cunningham) 27, (N Dickinson) 28;
Survival International (V Englebert) 20;
OSF (G I Bernard) 5,
J A L Cooke) 17; South American
Pictures (T Morrison) 3, 19,
(B Leimbach) 23; Zefa
(H Steenmans) 5.